WEIRD-BUT-TRUE FACTS ABOUT THE U.S. MILITARY

BY ARNOLD RINGSTAD · ILLUSTRATED BY KATHLEEN PETELINSEK

Published by The Child's World®
1980 Lookout Drive • Mankato, MN 56003-1705
800-599-READ • www.childsworld.com

Acknowledgments
The Child's World®: Mary Berendes, Publishing Director
Red Line Editorial: Editorial direction
The Design Lab: Design
Amnet: Production

ISBN 9781614734208
LCCN 2012946527

Printed in the United States of America
Mankato, MN
November, 2012
PA02143

About the Author

Arnold Ringstad lives in Minneapolis, Minnesota. He plans to build an aircraft carrier out of ice next winter.

About the Illustrator

Kathleen Petelinsek loves to draw and paint. She lives next to a lake in southern Minnesota with her husband, Dale; two daughters, Leah and Anna; two dogs, Gary and Rex; and her fluffy cat, Emma.

TABLE OF CONTENTS

INTRODUCTION

The United States military has been around since 1775. Many great soldiers, scientists, and leaders have served in the military since then. They have flown planes, steered ships, and won wars. They also have fought pirates, trained dolphins, and built aircraft carriers longer than three football fields. From weird weapons to bizarre battles, get ready to learn odd facts about the U.S. military—and remember, they are all true!

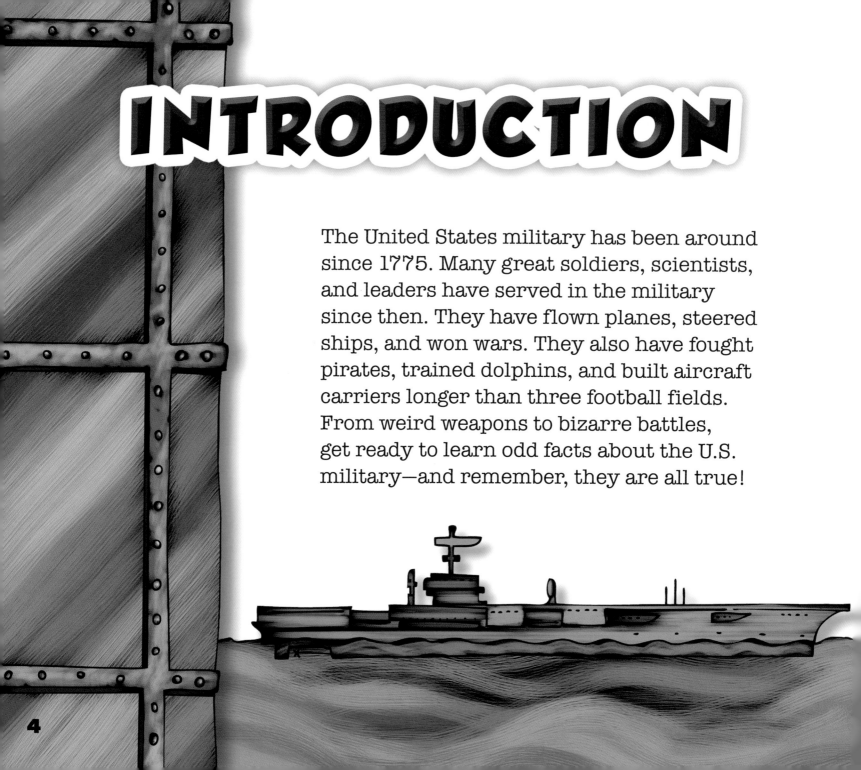

WEIRD WEAPONS

The first war submarine was used in 1776 during the American Revolution (1775–1783).

The *Turtle* looked like an egg with **propellers**. It attempted to sink British ships on three occasions but wasn't successful. It sunk when the ship transporting it went down under enemy fire later in 1776.

The U.S. military has invisible airplanes.

The planes are not invisible to the eye, but they can be very difficult to detect on radar. The shapes of the planes are designed to scatter radar signals, and special paint absorbs radar signals.

There were plans to drop bomb-carrying bats from airplanes during World War II (1939–1945) to destroy enemy cities.

The plan was never used. In testing, the bats were chilled so they would stay asleep. When they were released, they didn't wake up, so they fell to their deaths.

Pigeons were used in World War I (1914–1918) to send military messages.

The U.S. military uses trained dolphins to rescue swimmers and find underwater bombs.

Military dolphins use echolocation to find underwater mines.

During World War II, there were plans to make aircraft carriers out of ice.

The plans were cancelled because the ships would be too slow and expensive.

The U.S. military wants to build an airplane-mounted laser weapon.

It has spent 16 years and billions of dollars creating it. It costs almost $100,000 an hour to fly it. However, tests of the laser have been unsuccessful.

In the Vietnam War (1954–1975), the U.S. military made machines that could smell the enemy.

The machines detected ammonia, a chemical given off by unwashed bodies. The machines were put on helicopters and flown over places that were suspected of being enemy hideouts. However, the devices did not work very well, and the plan was abandoned.

In the 1850s, the U.S. military bought dozens of camels to make it easier to travel through the dry American West.

However, it turned out that the horses and camels did not work well together, so the military stopped using them.

MILITARY PEOPLE

After World War II, the "Candy Bomber" dropped candy to German children from his plane.

In 1948, the Soviet Union blocked roads to the capital city Berlin, preventing supplies from being delivered. The U.S. Air Force and other air forces decided to deliver food and fuel using airplanes instead. This was called the Berlin Airlift. One U.S. pilot who dropped candy from his plane was nicknamed the Candy Bomber.

The youngest **general** in U.S. history was **23 years old**.

George Armstrong Custer became a general in the Union army during the U.S. Civil War (1861–1865). In 1876, he led a cavalry expedition against the Lakota and Cheyenne. He and all his men were killed at the Battle of Little Bighorn.

By law, **George Washington will always be the highest-ranked officer in the United States military**.

Washington's highest rank during his lifetime was lieutenant general. He died in 1799. In 1976, Congress declared him General of the Armies of the United States. They also said that no other soldier, past or present, is ever allowed to outrank him.

General of the Armies of the United States

Twelve U.S. presidents served as generals before being elected as president.

They were: George Washington, Andrew Jackson, William Henry Harrison, Zachary Taylor, Franklin Pierce, Andrew Johnson, Ulysses S. Grant, Rutherford B. Hayes, James Garfield, Chester A. Arthur, Benjamin Harrison, and Dwight Eisenhower.

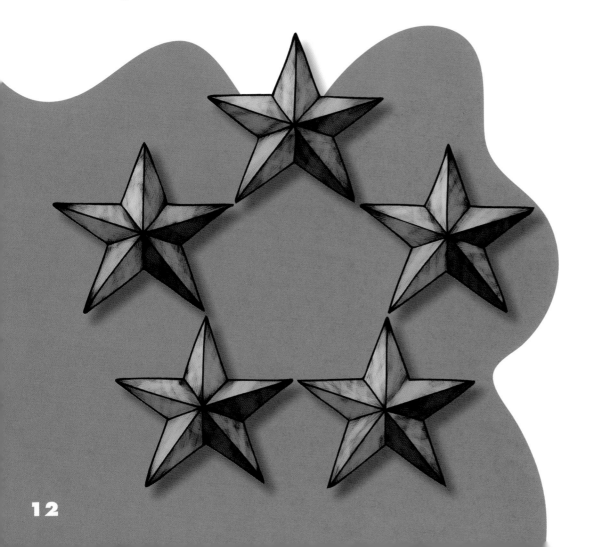

There have been only five 5-star U.S. Army generals.

Four of them were promoted to that rank within a one-week span in December 1944 during World War II.

A Revolutionary War ship captain later joined the Russian Navy.

John Paul Jones was a hero in the United States during and after the war. He joined the Russian Navy briefly in 1798 because he wanted experience commanding a fleet.

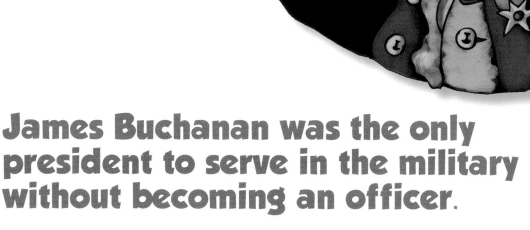

James Buchanan was the only president to serve in the military without becoming an officer.

He served as a private, the lowest military rank, in the War of 1812.

The last Revolutionary War **veteran** died in 1866.

The last Civil War veteran died in 1956, and the last World War I veteran died in 2011.

General Theodore Roosevelt Jr., the president's son, was in the first landing of the World War II D-Day invasion.

He was 57 years old and walked with a cane, but he insisted on landing with the first troops. Roosevelt was the only general to land with them.

REVOLUTIONARY WAR SOLDIER 1866

CIVIL WAR SOLDIER 1956

WORLD WAR I SOLDIER 2011

One World War II soldier was awarded 33 military medals and badges.

Audie Murphy was one of the most decorated soldiers in U.S. Army history. He later became a movie star.

The top U.S. fighter pilot in World War I shot down 22 planes and four observation balloons in six months.

Eddie Rickenbacker later became a race car driver and an airline executive.

BIG AND SMALL, LONG AND SHORT

The B-2 Bomber is the most expensive plane in the U.S. Air Force.

Each one costs more than 2 billion dollars.

The U.S. military spends more money than the next 14 countries' militaries combined.

The largest U.S. military base is almost 3,200 square miles (8,300 sq km).

White Sands **Missile** Range is bigger than the states of Rhode Island and Delaware combined.

The shortest officially declared war in U.S. history lasted only eight months.

The Spanish-American War began in April 1898 and ended in December of that year.

17

There are 17.5 miles (27 km) of hallways at the Pentagon, the main office building for the U.S. military.

The building has 131 stairways and 19 escalators.

The biggest ships in the U.S. Navy are more than 1,092 feet (305 m) long.

These are the *Nimitz*-class aircraft carriers. They are longer than three football fields and two times longer than the first aircraft carrier.

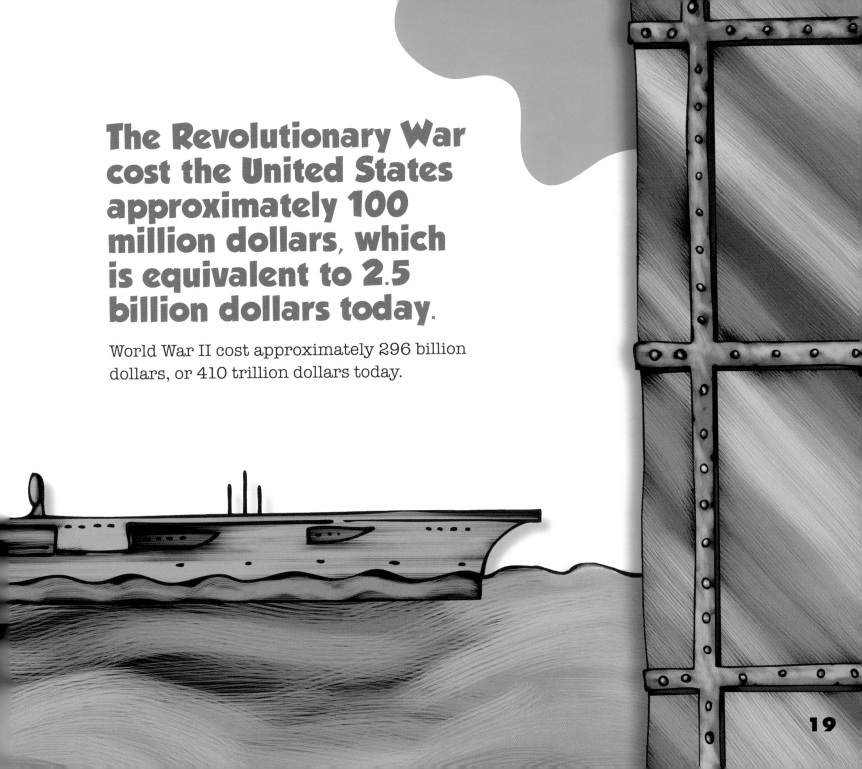

The Revolutionary War cost the United States approximately 100 million dollars, which is equivalent to 2.5 billion dollars today.

World War II cost approximately 296 billion dollars, or 410 trillion dollars today.

CURIOUS CONFLICTS

The U.S. military won every major battle in the Mexican-American War.

The war lasted from 1846 to 1848. It was the first U.S. war fought on foreign land. The Americans won all 11 major battles.

During one Civil War battle in September 1862, the Union commander stopped fighting so he could ask the Confederate commander what to do.

The Union commander did not want to waste his men's lives if fighting would be hopeless. The Confederate commander recommended that he surrender, and he did so. This happened at the Battle of Munfordville in Kentucky.

There was almost a rebellion over alcohol taxes in 1791.

Farmers protested the taxes and attacked the home of a tax collector. George Washington led an army of 13,000 soldiers to stop the protests.

The United States and Great Britain nearly went to war over a dead pig in 1859.

Both countries claimed the San Juan Islands, which are part of Washington State today. An American farmer shot his British neighbor's pig when it walked onto his property. A British officer threatened to arrest the Americans on the island. Warships from both sides were sent to the island. Troops occupied the island for 12 years but no shots were fired. Finally the British left the island to the Americans in 1872.

The U.S. military fought pirates in the early 1800s.

The Barbary Wars were fought against pirates in North Africa. These wars were among the first fought by the United States.

The British Army invaded Washington, DC, in the War of 1812.

They burned the White House, the U.S. Capitol, and many other buildings. The attack was in response to an earlier invasion of Canada by the U.S. military.

One Confederate ship kept sailing for months after the Civil War ended.

The captain of the *Shenandoah* continued on, sinking Union merchant ships in the Pacific Ocean. He finally surrendered in England, seven months after the war had ended. The *Shenandoah* was the only Confederate ship to sail all the way around the world.

In 1944, the U.S. Navy fought the largest sea battle in history.

The Battle of the Philippine Sea, fought against the Japanese Navy, involved 24 aircraft carriers, more than 150 other ships, and at least 1,500 aircraft.

23

MORE AMAZING MILITARY FACTS

It is against the rules for a male U.S. Army soldier to carry an umbrella while in his dress blue uniform.

U.S. Marine Corps officers carry swords as part of their dress uniforms.

A leader of the Ottoman Empire gave a sword to a Marine Corps officer after a battle in 1805. The sword has been part of Marine Corps tradition ever since.

The B-52 Bomber was introduced in 1954 and is still used today.

It is expected to be in use until the 2040s.

In 2002, the U.S. Army created a video game to recruit new soldiers and train current soldiers.

Thousands of tourists watched the U.S. military test atomic bombs near Las Vegas, Nevada, in the 1950s.

If you're in the military, your mustache may be measured.

In the U.S. Navy, a man may have a mustache, but each mustache hair can be no longer than 1/2 inch (1.3 cm).

In the Revolutionary War, a skilled soldier could reload and shoot his weapon once every 15 seconds.

Modern guns can fire at least 100 times in the same amount of time.

During World War II, Academy Awards were made of plaster.

The awards, which are given in honor of the best movies, were usually made of metal. During the war, painted plaster was used because people were saving metal for use in the war.

By the end of World War II, almost 8 percent of the U.S. population was in the military.

Nearly 11 million people out of about 140 million were serving at that time. Today, there are about 1.4 million people in the U.S. military, out of a population of approximately 310 million.

U.S. military pilots sitting in New Mexico can fly planes thousands of miles away.

Drone pilots fly remote control airplanes from an Air Force base in the United States. They can use the planes to drop bombs, fire missiles, or just take pictures.

There is a military base built into a mountain.

The Cheyenne Mountain Complex in Colorado is designed to withstand atomic bomb blasts.

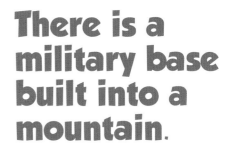

CHEYENNE MOUNTAIN OPERATIONS CENTER

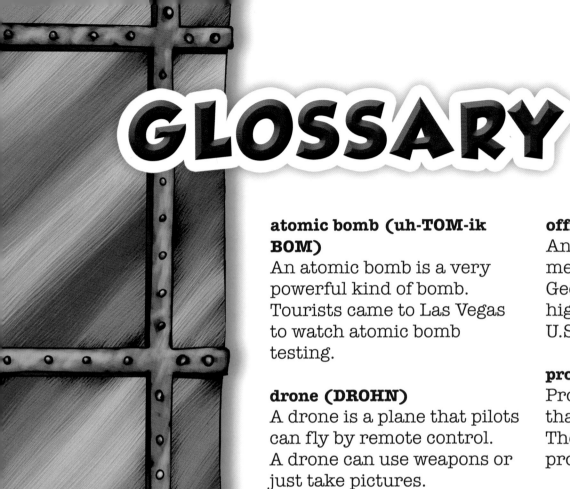

GLOSSARY

atomic bomb (uh-TOM-ik BOM)
An atomic bomb is a very powerful kind of bomb. Tourists came to Las Vegas to watch atomic bomb testing.

drone (DROHN)
A drone is a plane that pilots can fly by remote control. A drone can use weapons or just take pictures.

generals (JEN-ur-uls)
Generals are powerful military leaders. Several U.S. presidents were generals.

missile (MISS-ul)
A missile is a weapon that is shot at a target. A pilot can fire a missile at a target far away.

officer (OFF-uh-sur)
An officer is a high-ranking member of the military. George Washington is the highest-ranked officer in U.S. history.

propellers (pruh-PELL-urs)
Propellers are machines that push ships forward. The *Turtle* submarine had propellers to help it move.

veteran (VET-ur-un)
A veteran is a person who has retired from the military. There is no World War I veteran still living.

LEARN MORE

BOOKS

Lederer, Richard, and Caroline McCullagh. *American Trivia: What We All Should Know about U.S. History, Culture, and Geography.* Layton, UT: Gibbs Smith, 2012.

Marsh, Carole. *Civil War Trivia.* Peachtree City, GA: Gallopade International, 2010.

WEB SITES

Visit our Web site for links about weird U.S. military facts: **childsworld.com/links**

Note to Parents, Teachers, and Librarians: We routinely verify our Web links to make sure they are safe and active sites. So encourage your readers to check them out!

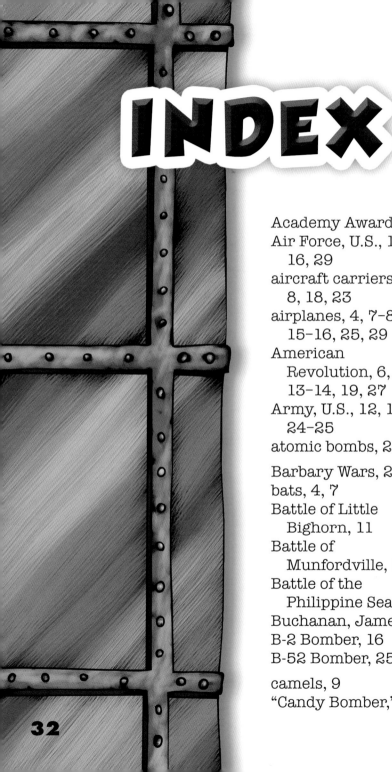

INDEX